I0617414

In the parliament of children
no one voted for war.

Kim Stafford

Fields *of* Peace

A Promise to Our Children

————

Copyright © 2023 / 2024
Fields of Peace / Charles P. Busch
All Rights Reserved

————

All rights reserved. No part of this publication may be reproduced, stored in an automated database, or made public in any form or by any means, electronically, mechanically, by photocopying, recording, or in any other way, without the prior written permission of the copyright holder.

ISBN: 979-8-9888993-6-5 - *softcover*

————

Book Design & Production
timmyroland.com

Fields *of* Peace

A Promise to Our Children

Charles P. Busch

Fields *of* Peace

FOREWORD

When my wife Cathey and I moved to Oregon 30 years ago, we became foster parents. Each girl and boy who came to live with us stole our hearts. And when they had to leave, broke our hearts.

One morning an infant boy, 16 days old, and premature, was delivered to our home. He had a little knit cap to keep his head warm, and was so tiny I could hold him in one hand. He was big-eyed and looked to me like a baby otter.

Within minutes, Cathey and I looked at one another. Yes. Somehow we both knew this one would stay, become ours.

In the weeks that followed, as I fed and changed and held him, I realized how little I had known about love. Though I had been preaching about it for years. How little I knew about love's vulnerability, and the tenderness which takes over. At night, when I tucked him in, I found myself singing to him. Not a lullaby, but a song from the musical Sweeney Todd:

> *Nothing's gonna harm you, not while I'm around . . .*
> *No one's gonna hurt you, no one's gonna dare . . .*
> *Others can desert you, not to worry, whistle I'll be there . . .*
> *Nothing's gonna harm you, not while I'm around . . .*

Fields *of* Peace
A Promise to Our Children

If you are a parent, you know what that song is about. By "parent" I include grandparent, God parent, foster parent, step-parent, aunt, uncle, caring neighbor, caring teacher, nurse, caring stranger.

With the arrival of the child who claims you, suddenly the world has a new center, and everything revolves around your wish for the well-being and future of that child. Everything! And the words, "Nothing's gonna harm you, not while I'm around," are sung with a catch in the throat, because you know that you will not always be around.

Surely this song is sung by every parent in every land, whatever the words, whatever the language. I like imagining the softness of those voices, and the ache behind the words. I also like to imagine the good that can come into the world if we chose to sing that song together.

Charles P. Busch
Founder, *Fields of Peace*
Coast of Oregon, 2023

Fields *of* Peace

A Promise to Our Children

I want to begin with a few ancient words.

> *Nations will beat their swords into plowshares,*
> *And their spears into pruning hooks.*
> *Nation shall not lift up sword against nation.*
> *Neither shall they learn war any more.*
>
> *Isaiah 2:4*

The Prophet Isaiah spoke these words nearly three thousand years ago. Yet, you and I know them, can almost recite them. Somehow they stayed in the air and been heard generation after generation.

Isaiah wasn't talking about the life to come, a heavenly realm, but peace among the nations of this world in time, in the course of human history.

I look to his words. I need their certainty, and what resolve I can take from them. Yet, each time I read them, I wonder, "When?" A hundred generations have passed since Isaiah's day, and still war follows war. In our day, some 40 wars.

Afghan Child

Fields *of* Peace

A Promise to Our Children

"When?" we ask. And know we are asking ourselves.

I am part of *Fields of Peace*, a nonprofit a few friends and I started 15 years ago on the coast of Oregon. Our name was inspired by this verse from the Sufi poet Jalal al-Din Rumi:

> *Out beyond ideas of wrongdoing and rightdoing, there is a field,*
> *I'll meet you there. When the soul lies down in that grass, the world*
> *is too full to talk about.   Ideas, language, even the phrase "*
> *each other" doesn't make any sense.*

That field is the world we wanted to help create. A world in which we meet having shed the ideologies and narratives by which we justify our oppression of others. A world in which we see that separateness is an illusion. See that we are connected, not only by obvious mutual interests, but by the threads of a marvelous web.

Our work was to teach the way of nonviolence: *Seeing each person as a beloved child of God.* Jesus's way. The way of Martin Luther King and Dorothy Day.

We conducted workshops, sent out a newsletter, and published a book of peace stories. These efforts continued for a decade. Then something happened. And it's that something I need to share with you this morning.

Iraqi Child

Fields *of* Peace
A Promise to Our Children

I received in the mail a bulletin from the Stanford University *News Service*. I have no idea who passed it on to me. It included a report on a panel discussion held there on "War and Ethics." One of the panelists was Richard Goldstone, a renowned jurist, and the first Chief Prosecutor at the International Criminal Court in the Hague. Goldstone offered this:

> **In World War I**, *the ratio of combatant deaths to civilian deaths was 9 to 1. For every 9 combatants killed, 1 civilian was killed.*

> **In World War II**, *the ratio changed dramatically. For every 1 combatant killed, 1 civilian was killed. A ratio of 1 to 1. Since then, he said, the numbers had again changed dramatically.*

> **In modern warfare**, *for every 1 combatant killed, 9 civilians are killed. A ratio of 1 to 9.*

So in the course of a hundred years, the very nature of war had changed. 9-to-1 had become 1-to-9.

I was stopped by this. How could I not be. Why hadn't I heard this before? Is it true? Has war become the killing of civilians?

Checking, I found that the 1 to 9 ratio had been reported consistently for the past three decades by U.N. agencies, Human Rights NGO's,

Syrian Child

and university peace study centers. It is true. Modern warfare is the killing of civilians, the majority of them children.

You and I see this confirmed daily in the headlines from the Ukraine War, Syrian War, Sudanese War, and the war on Palestine. Apartment buildings are targeted and bombed. And neighborhoods, hospitals, schools. And in the streets, snipers shoot fleeing mothers and children.

Modern warfare is the killing of civilians, most of them children.

To know this is to no longer be innocent. It is to be confronted by conscience. Conscience saying:

> *To kill a child is an absolute wrong.*
> *War has become the killing of children.*
> *Therefore, you must not be a part of war.*
> *Any war.*

What can we do? What can you and I do?

The answer that came to us at *Fields of Peace* was the obvious one: Start by making *A Promise to Our Children*. A Promise to not be a part of any war.

Palestinian Child

Fields *of* Peace
A Promise to Our Children

So we drafted a Promise.
A short one.
Only 48 words.

It begins,

***I will not be a part of the killing of any child,
no matter how lofty the reason.***

Leaders have to give reasons for the wars they want. The reasons follow a formula. Citizens are told that another nation is an imminent threat. That "they" want what we have. And we'll be safe only when "they" are obliterated. Good versus Evil, is always mentioned.

The explanations are kept short. The real appeal is to an unquestioning patriotism. I remember when our leaders decided to invade Iraq. We were told, "They have weapons of mass destruction aimed at us." What's needed is to bomb them, "Shock and Awe." That war lasted 20 years. No weapons of mass destruction were ever found. More than 300,000 Iraqi civilians were killed. Next, we added these words to the *Promise*:

***Not my neighbor's child. Not my child.
Not the enemy's child.***

Ukrainian Child

Fields *of* Peace
A Promise to Our Children

Down the street from my house is the Head Start School. Each morning a neighbor walks by with her little daughter. I love seeing them. They hold hands. Though I don't know her, I know the love that mother has for her daughter is the same as the love I have for my son, Gabriel. It is absolute. She would give her life for her child, as I would mine. Although I cannot look out the window and see my enemy walk by with his or her child, I know they too love their child, absolutely.

This beautiful, consuming, desperate love of parent for child is the same for people of every nation, whatever language they speak, whatever name they have for God. This is humanity's common ground. It is the field where we meet having shed our ideas about "the other." Standing together on this ground, our love for one child so easily becomes love for every child.

You and I have wondered how to love our enemy. Now we know. We hold their child as we hold our own.

The Promise ends with these words:

> *Not by bomb.*
> *Not by bullet.*
> *Not by looking the other way.*
> *I will be the power that is peace.*

Somalian Mother & Child

Fields *of* Peace
A Promise to Our Children

As citizens of the United States, you and I carry a particular burden. Our nation is a Military Empire, the Rome of our day.

> **Our Nation** maintains 800 military bases in foreign countries. Britain, France, and Russia combined have only 30 foreign bases.

> **Our Nation** starts big wars . . . Vietnam, Iraq, Afghanistan and is involved in nearly perpetual war.

> **Our Nation** is the gun store for the world. We sell by far the most weapons, tanks, fighter jets, bombs, missiles, to supply the wars of the world.

We are citizens of a Military Empire.   It is hard not to look the other way.

The last sentence of the *Promise* is . . . *I will be the power that is peace.* What is that power? It is the soft power of love at work in each of us: honesty, humility, forgiveness, compassion, a devotion to justice.

I know the 48-words of *A Promise to Our Children* may seem like nothing set against the machinery of war. The specter of war. But words have an inherent power. They hold the power of creation. But they must be said out loud.

Please join me in saying the *Promise* together:

Cameroonian Child

I will not be a part of the killing of any child,
no matter how lofty the reason.
Not my neighbor's child. Not my child.
Not the enemy's child.
Not by bomb. Not by bullet.
Not by looking the other way.
I will be the power that is peace.

15

Thank you. I hope you will step outside each morning and say the words of the *Promise* out loud. Birds will carry them, and clouds and breezes, and the Spirit itself. Like Isaiah's words, they will stay in the air and be heard.

Repeated, morning after morning, the words will also have their way with you. Change you. Move you to action. Make you "good trouble."

The Prophet Isaiah promised the time will come when, "Nation shall not lift up sword against nation."

Sudanese Child

Fields *of* Peace
A Promise to Our Children

When? Soon. Because our world has become too small, too connected, too mutually dependent, for the border-lessness of war.

When? Soon. Because the crises which now threaten human survival on our planet demand that nations unite in a common effort.

When? Soon. Because war has become self-annihilation, the killing of our children. Because we can no longer look the other way. Because the words of Isaiah's promise have now become *A Promise to Our Children.*

Afterword

IMAGINE yourself on an airport runway. It is early morning, barely light. You are wearing a pilot's jumpsuit, and behind you is a huge stealth bomber, black as a bat.

Standing with you is a five-year-old girl in a pink party dress. The two of you are alone. You don't know her and she doesn't know you. But she is looking up at you and she is smiling. Her face has a copper glow, and she is beautiful, utterly beautiful.

Inside your pocket is a cigarette lighter. Before you fly the plane, you've been ordered to do up close what you will do later in the day to children from 30 thousand feet. You are to set her dress on fire, set her on fire. You've been told the reason. It's a lofty one.

You kneel, and look up. The girl is curious, still smiling. You take out the lighter. She has no idea. It helps you not to know her name.

But you cannot do it. Of course you can't.

Addendum

The Convention on the Rights of Children was ratified by the General Assembly of the United Nations in 1990. It extended and further articulates the entitlement of children to "special care and assistance" stated in the *Geneva Declaration of the Rights of the Child* (1924), and the *Universal Declaration of Human Rights* (1948).

The Convention on the Rights of Children has been ratified by 196 nations, including every member of the United Nations, <u>with one exception</u>: The United States of America.

From the 54 Articles of The Convention

Article 6: States Parties recognize that every child has the inherent right to life. States Parties shall ensure to the maximum extent possible the survival and development of the child.

Article 19: States Parties shall take all appropriate legislative, administrative, social and educational measures to protect the child from all forms of physical or mental violence, injury or abuse, neglect or negligent treatment, maltreatment or exploitation, including sexual abuse, while in the care of parents, legal guardians, or any other person who has the care of the child.

Addendum

Article 22: States Parties shall take appropriate measures to ensure that a child who is seeking refugee status or who is considered a refugee . . . shall receive appropriate protection and humanitarian assistance . . .

Article 37: No child shall be subjected to torture or other cruel, inhuman or degrading treatment or punishment...

Article 38: States Parties undertake to respect and to ensure respect for rules of international humanitarian law applicable to them in armed conflicts which are relevant to the child. States Parties shall take all feasible measures to ensure that persons who have not attained the age of fifteen years do not take a direct part in hostilities . . . In accordance with their obligations under international humanitarian law to protect the civilian population in armed conflicts. State Parties shall take all feasible measures to ensure protection and care of children who are affected by an armed conflict.

Article 39: States Parties shall take all appropriate measures to promote physical and psychological recovery and social reintegration of a child victim of any form of neglect, exploitation, or abuse; torture or any other form of cruel inhuman or degrading treatment or punishment; or armed conflicts.

Credits / Thanks

Design, Layout & Production: Tim Gilman, timmyroland.com

Editing: Cathey Busch, Rod de Luca

Readers: Reem Ghunaim, Exec. Director, *Fields of Peace*
        & Ryan Gallagher, Board Chair

Foreword: "Not While I'm Around," lyrics by Steven Sondheim,
        from *Sweeney Todd*

Fields of Peace:
- Scripture: Isaiah 2:4
- Jalaluddin Rumi quote: "The Essential Rumi," translated by
Coleman Barks and John Moyne, HarperCollins, 1995
- Ratio of Combatant to Civilian in modern warfare:
The Stanford / News Service, Jan. 24, 2011.
A recent reference: U.N. Security Council Meeting,
May 25, 2022 (SC/14904), "Ninety Per Cent of War-Time
Casualties are Civilians."

Addendum: U.N. Convention on the Rights of the Child,
        Nov. 20, 1989

about Fields of Peace

We are moved by the fact that modern warfare has become the killing of civilians, the majority of them children.

Our mission is to build a global movement to safeguard the lives and welfare of children threatened by wars and conflict violence.

We begin by inviting each person to join us in making A Promise to Our Children---a 48-word pledge to abstain from contributing to the killing of any child by supporting war.

Our ongoing programs in East Africa and pending programs in the Middle East serve children of conflict impacted by war. We nurture their resilience, and empower them to lead the way to peace in their homeland and across borders through our movement.

We work toward a world in which conflicts are solved through nonviolent means, a world in which children have their basic rights and live in a world without war. Reflecting the beautiful sentiment articulated by Queen Rania of Jordan: *Peace means our children can sleep to a mother's soft voice, not screaming sirens, play with building blocks, not watch their homes destroyed; make friends, not lose them; dream of big plans for the future, not wonder if they would have one.*

For funding, we rely on a growing circle of friends and foundations. We need and ask for your personal support: *fieldsofpeace.org*

Reem Ghunaim, *Executive Director* / **Charles Busch**, *Founder*

Board Members

Lydia Asana-Ngua / Florida
Ryan Gallagher *Chair* / Hawaii
Bior Garang / Kenya
Wayne Martin / Oregon
Michael Osterer / New York
Martha Payne *Treasure* / Oregon
Annabelle Schwartz *Secretary* / New York

Artist in Residence

William Kucha / Painter, Sculptor, Singer / Songwriter,
Friend of the Earth

Advisory Board

Suman Aggarwal, PhD / Founder & President,
Shanti Sahyog Center for Nonviolence, India
Rod DeLuca / Former Chair of the Board
Alex del Vecchio / Peace Village Committee
Patrick Hiller, PhD / Director, War Prevention Initiative
James Owaka / Center for Nonviolence-Africa
Kim Stafford / Poet
David Swanson / Founder & Director, World Beyond War

www.ingramcontent.com/pod-product-compliance
Lightning Source LLC
Chambersburg PA
CBHW041622120626
46551CB00003B/553